TREES

APPLE TREES

John F. Prevost
ABDO & Daughters

Published by Abdo & Daughters, 4940 Viking Drive, Suite 622, Edina, Minnesota 55435.

Copyright © 1996 by Abdo Consulting Group, Inc., Pentagon Tower, P.O. Box 36036, Minneapolis, Minnesota 55435 USA. International copyrights reserved in all countries. No part of this book may be reproduced in any form without written permission from the publisher.

Printed in the United States.

Cover Photo credits: Peter Arnold, Inc.
Interior Photo credits: Peter Arnold, Inc.

Edited by Bob Italia

Library of Congress Cataloging-in-Publication Data

Prevost, John F.
    Apple Trees / John F. Prevost.
      p. cm. -- (Trees)
    Includes index.
    Summary: Presents brief information about the roots, trunk, leaves, fruits, and varieties of apple trees, pests that affect them, their economic uses, and more.
     ISBN 1-56239-614-5
    1. Apples--Juvenile literature. [1. Apples. 2. Trees.] I. Title. II. Series: Prevost, John F. Trees.
QK495.R78P73 1996   96-310
583'.372 –dc20   CIP
                                                                                        AC

ABOUT THE AUTHOR
John Prevost is a marine biologist and diver who has been active in conservation and education issues for the past 18 years. Currently he is living inland and remains actively involved in freshwater and marine husbandry, conservation and education projects.

Contents

Apple Trees and Family 4
Roots, Soil, and Water 6
Stems, Leaves, and Sunlight 8
Flowers, Fruit, and Seeds 10
Insects and Other Friends 12
Pests and Diseases 14
Varieties 16
Uses 18
Apple Trees and the Plant Kingdom ... 20
Glossary 22
Index 24

Apple Trees and Family

Apple trees are the most popular fruit trees. They are grown in **temperate climates**. Their leaves fall in autumn.

Apple trees were developed thousands of years ago in southern Europe and central Asia. Apple trees reached North America with the early European settlers in the 1600s.

Apple trees, pear trees, and crabapple trees make up the apple tree **family**. Apple trees are grown for their fruit and flowers. The crabapple tree is among the prettiest spring **bloomers**. Some apple tree **varieties** feed birds and **mammals** in the fall and winter.

Apple trees grow over more parts of the Earth than any other fruit tree.

5

Roots, Soil, and Water

Most apple trees have two parts. The **scion** is the top that branches and bears fruit. It is **grafted** onto a **rootstock**. The rootstock can be a **seedling**, which makes a full-size or standard tree.

The rootstock also can be **dwarfing**, which makes a tree that is smaller than full-size. The rootstock determines the tree's size. It does not affect the fruit type.

Rootstocks also can control the time the tree makes fruit. Many rootstock types come from crabapple trees.

Apple trees will grow in most soils. But they need good **drainage**. In wet areas, roots will die.

The scion is the top part of the tree that branches and bears fruit.

Stems, Leaves, and Sunlight

The tree **trunk** holds up the branches, stems, and leaves. Sunlight is important because it is used to change water, **nutrients**, and air into food and **oxygen**. This process is called **photosynthesis**.

The trunk, branches, and stems connect the leaves to the roots. They send water and nutrients from the roots to the leaves. Food made by the leaves then returns to the roots.

Apple tree leaves grow singly on the **twigs**. They are often round or narrow with jagged edges. The leaves' undersides are covered with pale, soft hairs.

Photosynthesis

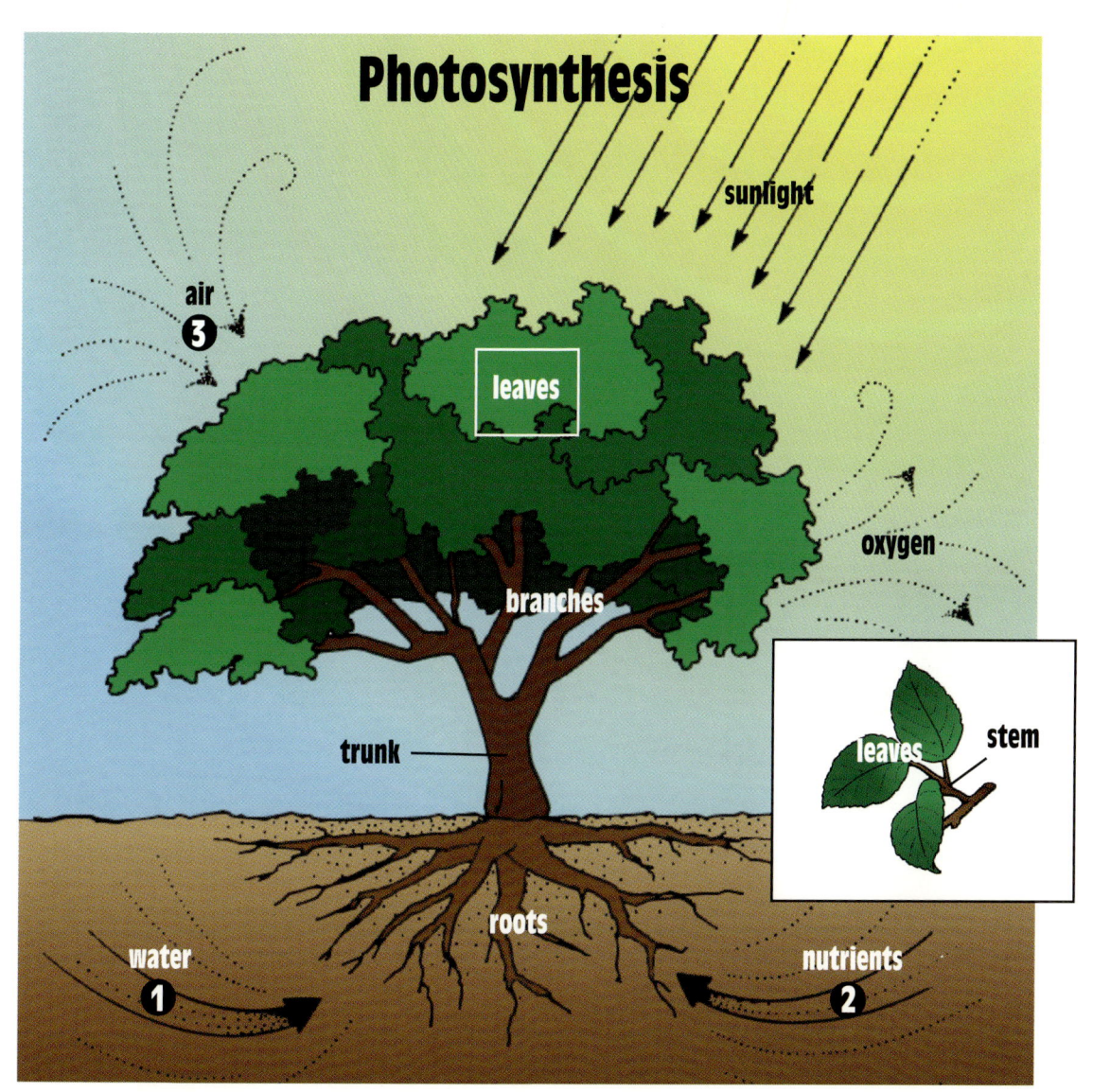

Ground water (1) and nutrients (2) travel through the roots, trunk, and branches and into the leaves where air (3) is drawn in. Then the tree uses sunlight to change these three elements into food and oxygen.

9

Flowers, Fruit, and Seeds

Apple trees **bloom** from April to mid-May. Apple **blossoms** have **petals** and a strong, sweet smell. Their colors range from white to red.

Apple trees have flowers to make fruit. Fruit grows in the **pistil's ovary** after **pollen** from the **stamen fertilizes** the flower.

Inside each grown apple are the seeds. Each seed contains an **embryo** which can grow into a tree. When the apples and seeds fall to the ground, the growing process can begin.

BLOSSOMS

petal, pistil, pollen, stamen, ovary

APPLE

seeds

Pollen from the stamen fertilizes the pistil's ovary which grows into an apple. Each apple contains seeds which carry tiny plant embryos.

11

Insects and Other Friends

The color and smell of the flower attract insects such as bees, which land on the **petals.** The flower's sweet **nectar** rewards each insect with a small meal. **Pollen** sticks to the insects while they feed. These insects then carry pollen from flower to flower, **pollinating** the apple tree.

Apple trees also are home for other types of insects, spiders, and **mites.** Many are **predators** that eat **pests** which often damage trees.

Apple trees also provide homes for birds which build nests in the branches. Birds help the tree by feeding on pests.

Opposite page:
The color and smell of the flower invites insects to land on the petals.

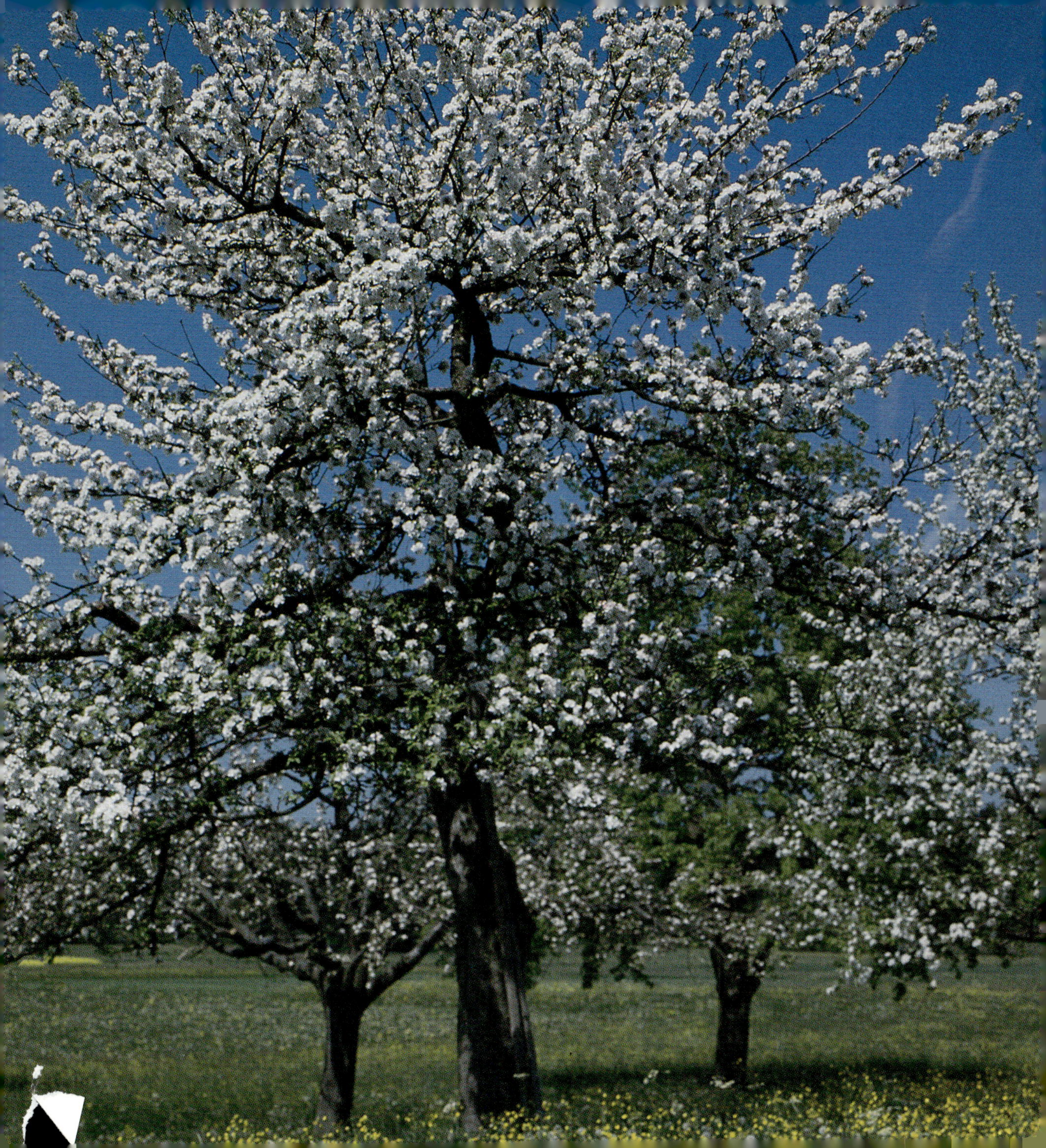

Pests and Diseases

Pests such as **aphids**, **mites**, and hornets are a major problem of apple growing. At least 25 types of insects attack apple trees in all parts of North America. They may be controlled with oil, sprays, **predatory** insects, or **chemicals**. This is why apples should be washed before they are eaten.

Diseases also attack apple trees. Apple scab, cedar apple rust, and fire blight are diseases that can kill these trees. **Poison** is often sprayed on apple trees to fight diseases.

Mice, rabbits, and deer can be pests. These **mammals** will chew the bark and eat the **twigs** off of a tree. A wire mesh sleeve placed around the **trunk** keeps away rabbits and mice. Deer must be scared away or they will eat the tree.

Apple growers must control pests and diseases to protect their crop.

15

Varieties

There are over 6,000 apple tree **varieties** in the world. Any two are needed for fruit production, but they must **bloom** at the same time.

Some varieties make **sterile pollen** and are not used to **pollinate** other trees. Pollen from golden delicious, grimes golden, jonathan, and winter banana are excellent.

Fruit size ranges from under 1 inch (2.5 cm) to over 7 inches (18 cm) depending on the variety. Younger trees will have larger fruit than older trees.

There are thousands of apple varieties, but only a few are good to eat.

Uses

Apple trees are grown for their fruit and beauty. They are one of the first trees to **blossom** each spring. There is a large industry supporting the **grafting** and growing of apple trees for home and **agricultural** use.

Wood workers use apple trees to make furniture. The wood is obtained from full-sized trees in older **orchards**. These trees are no longer making fruit and are at the end of their **lifespan**.

An apple farm in New York.

Apple Trees and the Plant Kingdom

The plant kingdom is divided into several groups, including flowering plants, fungi, plants with bare seeds, and ferns.

Flowering plants grow flowers to make seeds. These seeds often grow inside protective ovaries or fruit.

Fungi are plants without leaves, flowers, or green coloring, and cannot make their own food. They include mushrooms, molds, and yeast.

Plants with bare seeds (such as evergreens or conifers) do not grow flowers. Their seeds grow unprotected, often on the scale of a cone.

Ferns are plants with roots, stems, and leaves. They do not grow flowers or seeds.

There are two groups of flowering plants: monocots (MAH-no-cots) and dicots (DIE-cots). Monocots have seedlings with one leaf. Dicots have seedlings with two leaves.

The rose family is one type of dicot. Apple trees belong to the rose family.

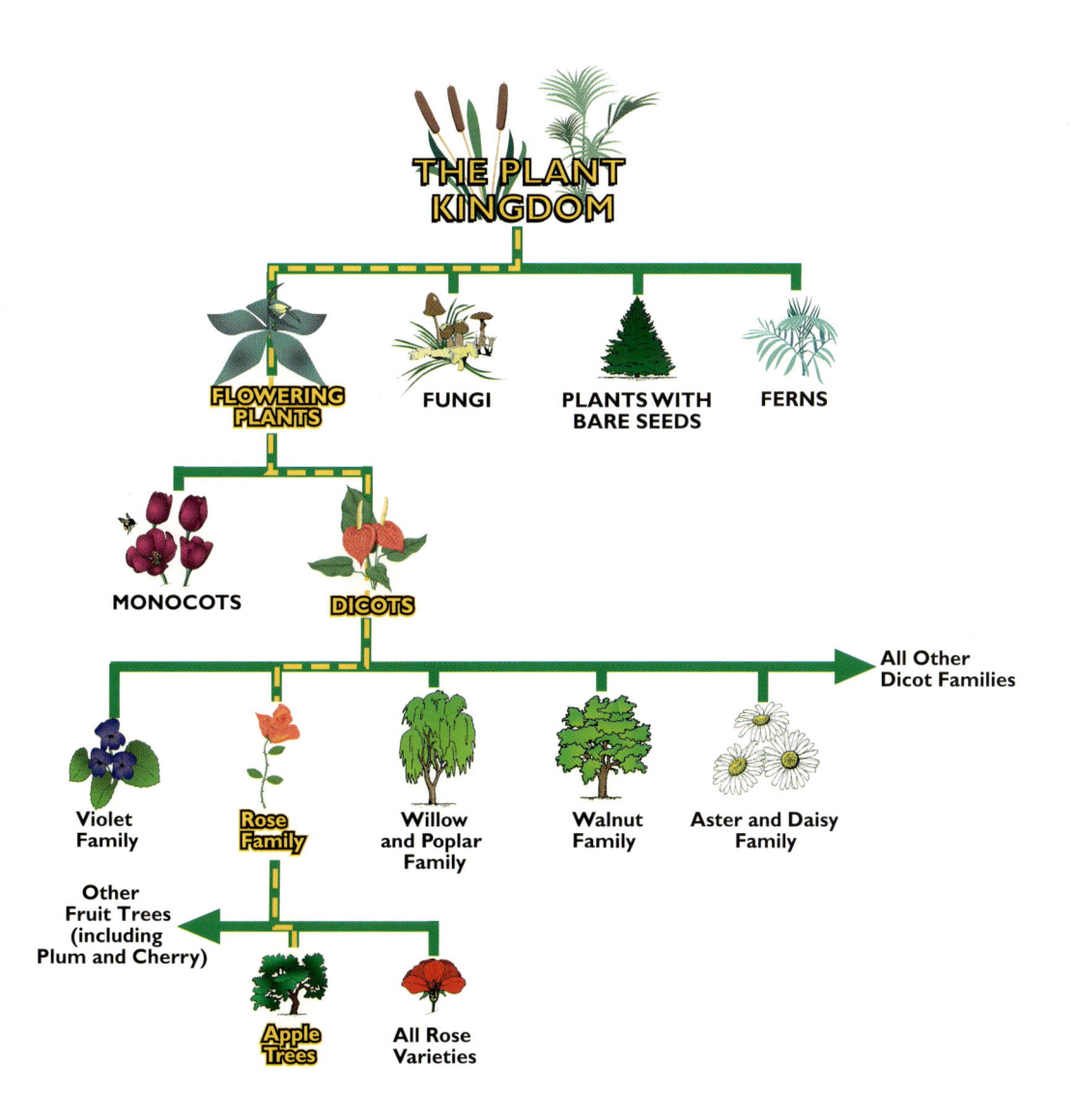

THE PLANT KINGDOM

- FLOWERING PLANTS
  - MONOCOTS
  - DICOTS
    - Violet Family
    - Rose Family
      - Other Fruit Trees (including Plum and Cherry)
      - Apple Trees
      - All Rose Varieties
    - Willow and Poplar Family
    - Walnut Family
    - Aster and Daisy Family
    - All Other Dicot Families
- FUNGI
- PLANTS WITH BARE SEEDS
- FERNS

Glossary

agriculture (AG-rih-kull-chur) - The raising of crops and farm animals.

aphid (AY-fid) - A small insect that sucks the sap from plant leaves and stems.

bloom - To have flowers; also, a flower blossom.

blossom (BLAH-sum) - The flower of a plant.

chemical (KEM-ih-kull) - A substance used to create a reaction or process.

climate (KLIE-mat) - The type of weather a place has.

disease (diz-EEZ) - A sickness.

drainage (DRAIN-ij) - The removal of water from soil by pipes or slope of soil.

dwarf - A plant much smaller than the usual size for its kind.

embryo (EM-bree-oh) - An early stage of plant growth, before sprouting from a seed.

family - A group of related living things.

fertile (FIR-tull) - To be able to produce growth or offspring.

graft - To connect a bud or stem of one plant into another plant and have it grow.

lifespan - How long a thing lives.

mammals - A class of animals, including humans, that have hair and feed their young milk.

mite - A tiny animal related to the spider and has eight legs.

nectar - The sweet fluid produced by flowers to attract pollinating insects.

nutrient (NOO-tree-ent) - Substance that promotes growth or good health.

orchard - The area of ground where trees are grown.

ovary - The part of a plant where seeds are made.
oxygen (OX-ih-jen) - A gas without color, taste, or odor found in air and water.
pest - A harmful or destructive insect.
petal - One of several leaves that protect the flower's center.
photosynthesis (foe-toe-SIN-thuh-sis) - Producing food using sunlight as the source of energy.
pistil (PIS-tull) - The female (seed-making) flower part.
poison (POY-zun) - A substance that is dangerous to life or health.
pollen (PAH-lin) - A yellow powder that fertilizes flowers.
pollinate (PAH-lin-ate) - To move pollen from flower to flower, allowing them to develop seeds.
predator (PRED-uh-tor) - An animal that eats other animals.
rootstock - The underground portion of a plant.
scion (SIGH-un) - A cutting, bud, or twig that is grafted to another plant.
seedling - A young plant grown from a seed.
stamen (STAY-men) - The male flower part (OR the flower part that makes pollen).
sterile (STAIR-ul) - To be unable to produce fruit.
temperate (TEM-prit) - Not too hot and not too cold.
trunk - The main stem of a tree, from which branches and roots grow.
twig - A very small branch of a tree.
varieties (vuh-RYE-uh-tees) - Different types of plants that are closely related.

Index

A
agriculture 18
air 8
aphids 14
apple trees 20
apples 10, 18
Asia 4
autumn 4

B
bees 12
birds 4, 12
bloom 10
bloomers 4
blossoms 10, 18
branches 6, 8

C
chemicals 14
climate 4
color 10, 12, 13
cones 20
conifers 20
crabapple trees 6
crabapples 4

D
deer 14
dicots 20
diseases 14
drainage 6
dwarf 6

E
embryo 10
Europe 4
European settlers 4
evergreens 20

F
family 4
ferns 20

fertilization 10
flowering plants 20
flowers 4, 10, 20
food 8, 20
fruit 4, 6, 16, 18, 20
fruit trees 4, 20
fungi 20

G
grafting 6, 18

I
industry 18
insects 12, 14

L
leaves 4, 8, 20
lifespan 18

M
mammals 4, 14
mice 14
mites 14
molds 20
monocots 20
mushrooms 20

N
nectar 12
North America 4, 14
nutrients 8

O
orchards 18
ovaries 10, 20
oxygen 8

P
pears 4
pests 12, 14
petals 10, 12

photosynthesis 8
pistil 10
plant kingdom 20
poison 14
pollen 10, 12, 16
pollination 12
predators 12, 14

R
rabbits 14
roots 6, 8, 20
rootstock 6
rose family 20

S
scion 6
seedlings 6
seeds 10, 20
smell 10, 12
soil 6
spiders 12
stamen 10
stems 8, 20
sunlight 8

T
trunk 8, 14
twigs 8

V
varieties 4, 16

W
water 8
winter 4, 16

Y
yeast 20